# Mandala Coloring Book:

# 54

Unique and Highly Detailed
Mandalas for Adult Relaxation,
Stress Management, Concentration,
and Mandala Meditation

Kameliya Angelkova

# DEDICATION

I dedicate this coloring book to all people who enjoy art, meditation, and coloring in general. It is ideal for those who want enrich their coloring book library or give as a gift to adults, office colleagues, or teenagers. It contains a bunch of highly detailed, intricate, unique, and beautiful mandala designs: a hundred percent original artwork!

# FEATURES OF THIS BOOK:

54 unique, intricate, highly detailed mandalas
6 preview pages included
Professionally illustrated designs – all – original artwork
Various types of mandalas: floral, animal, solar, geometric, abstract
All circular in shape
Guarantees hours of joy, relaxation, creativity, and concentration
Suitable for colored pencils, crayons, pastels.
All mandalas are one-sided print
NO duplicates
NO thick lines
NO filled in areas
NO gray shades
NO grayscale areas

# PREVIEW PAGE #1

On the back side of the page:

Preview page one, which includes nine samples of all the 54 mandala designs

# PREVIEW PAGE #2

On the back side of the page:

Preview page two, which includes nine more mandala designs

# PREVIEW PAGE #3

On the back side of the page:

Preview page three, which includes nine more mandala designs

# PREVIEW PAGE #4

On the back side of the page:

Preview page four, which includes nine more mandala designs

# PREVIEW PAGE #5

On the back side of the page:

Preview page five, which includes nine more mandala designs

# PREVIEW PAGE #6

On the back side of the page:

Preview page six, which includes nine more mandala designs

On the back side of the page:

#1 Highly-detailed floral mandala design

On the back side of the page:

#2 Highly detailed abstract mandala design

On the back side of the page:

#3 Highly detailed abstract mandala design

On the back side of the page:

#4 Highly detailed abstract mandala design with small butterflies

On the back side of the page:

#5 Highly detailed floral mandala design with small elephant heads and lotuses

On the back side of the page:

#6 Highly detailed abstract mandala design with peacock feathers

On the back side of the page:

#7 Highly detailed solar mandala design with suns and moons

On the back side of the page:

#8 Highly detailed abstract mandala design with stylized plants

On the back side of the page:

#9 Highly detailed floral mandala design with small tiger heads

On the back side of the page:

#10 Highly detailed rose mandala design with stylized petals

On the back side of the page:

#11 Highly detailed Eastern mandala design with the yin and yang symbol

On the back side of the page:

#12 Highly detailed solar mandala design with sun and rays

On the back side of the page:

#13 Highly detailed mandala design lion head, masks, and plants

On the back side of the page:

#14 Highly detailed floral mandala design

On the back side of the page:

#15 Highly detailed abstract mandala design with stylized peacock feathers and floral elements

On the back side of the page:

#16 Highly detailed floral mandala design

On the back side of the page:

#17 Highly detailed mandala design with arrows and feathers

On the back side of the page:

#18 Highly detailed floral mandala design

On the back side of the page:

#19 Highly detailed marine mandala design with seashells, fish, and sea stars

On the back side of the page:

#20 Highly detailed romantic mandala design with hearts

On the back side of the page:

#21 Highly detailed vintage mandala design with vines

On the back side of the page:

#22 Highly detailed floral mandala design with apples and apple trees

On the back side of the page:

#23 Highly detailed spider web mandala design with a spider, butterflies, and some dragonflies

On the back side of the page:

#24 Highly detailed floral mandala design

On the back side of the page:

#25 Highly detailed moon mandala design with the moon phases

On the back side of the page:

#26 Highly detailed marine mandala design with sea creatures

On the back side of the page:

#27 Highly detailed floral mandala design

On the back side of the page:

#28 Highly detailed abstract mandala design

On the back side of the page:

#29 Highly detailed geometric mandala design

On the back side of the page:

#30 Highly detailed mandala design with feathers and birds

On the back side of the page:

#31 Highly detailed fire mandala design

On the back side of the page:

#32 Highly detailed floral mandala design

On the back side of the page:

#33 Highly detailed butterfly mandala design with flowers and smaller butterflies

On the back side of the page:

#34 Highly detailed abstract mandala design

On the back side of the page:

#35 Highly detailed Egypt style mandala design with eye and papyrus plants

On the back side of the page:

#36 Highly detailed floral mandala design with four-leaf clovers

On the back side of the page:

#37 Highly detailed butterfly mandala design (second version)

On the back side of the page:

#38 Highly detailed abstract mandala design floral elements

On the back side of the page:

#39 Highly detailed vintage mandala design with fine vines

On the back side of the page:

#40 Highly detailed elephant mandala design with floral elements

On the back side of the page:

#41 Highly detailed abstract mandala design with stylized birds

On the back side of the page:

#42 Highly detailed abstract mandala design with floral elements

On the back side of the page:

#43 Highly detailed geometric mandala design with circles

On the back side of the page:

#44 Highly detailed floral mandala design with leafs

On the back side of the page:

#45 Highly detailed floral mandala design with petals

On the back side of the page:

#46 Highly detailed floral mandala design

ABOUT THE AU On the back side of the page:

#47 Highly detailed mandala design with a crane, some rush, and some feathers

On the back side of the page:

#48 Highly detailed abstract mandala design

On the back side of the page:

#49 Highly detailed abstract mandala design

On the back side of the page:

#50 Highly detailed abstract mandala design with small suns

On the back side of the page:

#51 Highly detailed mandala design with a stylized snowflake

On the back side of the page:

#52 Highly detailed romantic mandala design with small hearts

On the back side of the page:

#53 Highly detailed mandala design with a Gorgon Medusa head and snakes

# ABOUT THE AUTHOR

Kameliya Angelkova is a European author and designer who writes her books with much love. She is a fan of uplifting books, positive thinking, graphic and motion graphic design, and of course – writing! She also likes eating and cooking healthy homemade meals. Starting as an independent author, she has the enormous desire to present to her readers some interesting, motivational and useful books.
Check the other books of this author for more inspiration and daily positive energy on the author's page on Amazon!

Made in the USA
Middletown, DE
07 January 2021